Nitrogen

and the Group 5 Elements

THE PERIODIC TABLE

Nigel Saunders

Heinemann
LIBRARY

www.heinemann.co.uk/library

Visit our website to find out more information about Heinemann Library books.

To order:

 Phone 44 (0) 1865 888066

 Send a fax to 44 (0) 1865 314091

 Visit the Heinemann Bookshop at www.heinemann.co.uk/library to browse our catalogue and order online.

First published in Great Britain by Heinemann Library, Halley Court, Jordan Hill, Oxford OX2 8EJ, part of Harcourt Education. Heinemann is a registered trademark of Harcourt Education Ltd.

Produced for Heinemann by Discovery Books Ltd.

Editorial: Dr Carol Usher and Sarah Eason
Design: Ian Winton
Illustrations: Peter Bull and Stefan Chabluk
Picture Research: Vashti Gwynn
Production: Edward Moore

Originated by Ambassador Litho Ltd
Printed and bound in Hong Kong, China by South China Printing Company

ISBN 0 431 16996 9
08 07 06 05 04
10 9 8 7 6 5 4 3 2 1

British Library Cataloguing in Publication Data
Saunders, N. (Nigel)
  Nitrogen and the group 5 elements. –
  - (The periodic table)
  546.7'1
A full catalogue record for this book is available from the British Library.

Acknowledgements
The publishers would like to thank the following for permission to reproduce photographs:
Terry Benson p39; Corbis pp4, 25 (Neal Preston), 8 (Tom Stewart), 11 (Martyn Goddard), 14 (Bob Winsett), 19, 34 (Hulton-Deutsch Collection), 21 (Robert Pickett), 26 (Bettmann), 35 (Leif Skoogfors), 41 top (C/B Productions), 42 (Maurice Nimmo, Frank Lane Picture Agency), 47 (Francis G Mayer), 50 (Randy Faris), 52 (Lester V Bergman), 54 (Dale C Spartas), 56 (Jose Luis Pelaez), 57 (Gary Kufner); Science Photo Library pp9 (Ed Young, Agstock), 12, 15 (Mauro Fermariello), 17 (Cordelia Molloy), 18, (Andrew Lambert Photography), 23, 24, (Charles D Winters), 27 (Martyn F Chilmaid), 28 (P Sole, ISM), 29, 32, 33 (Roberto De Gugliemo), 37 (Michael Marten), 38 (Manfred Kage), 41 bottom, 43 (Sinclair Stammers), 44 (D Boone), 45 (Hank Morgan), 48 top (Russ Lappa), 48 bottom (Ric Ergenbright), 51 (NIBSC).

Cover photograph of lightning storm, reproduced with permission of Corbis. Lightning fixes nitrogen in the atmosphere.

The author would like to thank Angela, Kathryn, David and Jean for all their help and support.

Contents

Words appearing in bold, **like this**, are explained in the Glossary

Elements and atomic structure

There are different chemicals everywhere you look. The food you eat, the air you breathe and the water you drink are all made from them. In fact, you and everything in your surroundings are made from chemicals. Most chemicals are solids, but some are gases, such as the air and others are liquids, such as water. All chemicals have one thing in common; whether they are simple or complex – they are made from just a few simple substances called **elements**.

Elements and compounds

Elements are chemicals that cannot be broken down into anything simpler using chemical **reactions**. There are about ninety naturally occurring elements and scientists have learned how to make over twenty more using **nuclear reactions**. More than three-quarters of the elements are metals, such as aluminium and iron, while the rest are non-metals, like nitrogen and phosphorus. Elements join together in chemical reactions to make **compounds**. Magnesium and nitrogen, for example, can react to make magnesium nitride. Nearly all the millions of chemicals in the world are compounds, made up of two or more elements chemically joined together.

▼ *Everything you can see here, including the circus performers and their colourful clothing, is made from some of the innumerable chemical compounds and elements in the world.*

Atoms

All chemicals, including elements and compounds, are made up of tiny particles called **atoms**. Elements contain only one sort of atom, while compounds are made from two or more types of atom joined together. Although we can see most of the chemicals around us, individual atoms are not visible, even with a light microscope. Bismuth has quite large atoms compared with other elements, but you would need to make an atom of bismuth six hundred and seventy million times larger for it to be as big as a soccer ball!

Subatomic particles

Atoms are made from even smaller objects called **subatomic particles**. At the centre of each atom there is a **nucleus**, which contains **protons** and **neutrons**. These are the largest subatomic particles. Protons are positively charged while neutrons have no charge. Smaller, negatively-charged subatomic particles, called **electrons**, are arranged in layers or 'shells' around the nucleus. This arrangement of electrons resembles the way the planets are arranged around the Sun. Actually, most of an atom is empty space.

neutron   proton

nucleus

electron

This is a model of a nitrogen atom. Each one contains 7 protons and 7 neutrons, with 7 electrons arranged in two shells or energy levels around the nucleus.

Groups

With so many elements to study, chemists needed to organize them so they could understand the different chemical reactions they were observing. Several people tried to do this, but a Russian chemist called Dimitri Mendeleev made the best attempt. In 1869, he formed a table, where each element was placed into one of eight **groups**. Each group contained elements with similar chemical properties. This made it much easier for chemists to predict what might happen when elements reacted with each other. Mendeleev's table was so successful that the modern **periodic table** is based closely on it.

CHAPTER 2

The periodic table, nitrogen and group 5

The modern **periodic table** has developed from Mendeleev's table. Each vertical column in the periodic table is called a **group** and there are eighteen groups altogether. The **elements** in a group have similar chemical properties to each other. The horizontal rows are called **periods**. The number of **protons** in the **nucleus** of each **atom** (called the **atomic number**) increases from left to right across a period and as you go down a group.

The number of **electrons** in an atom and how they are arranged in their shells determines how an element **reacts**. Each element in a group has the same number of electrons in its outer shell. This is the shell furthest from the **nucleus**. The elements in group 1 all have one electron in their outer shells, whereas those in group 5 have five. The periodic table gets its name because different chemical properties are repeated regularly or periodically.

The properties of the elements change gradually as you go down a group. For instance, the elements in group 7 become

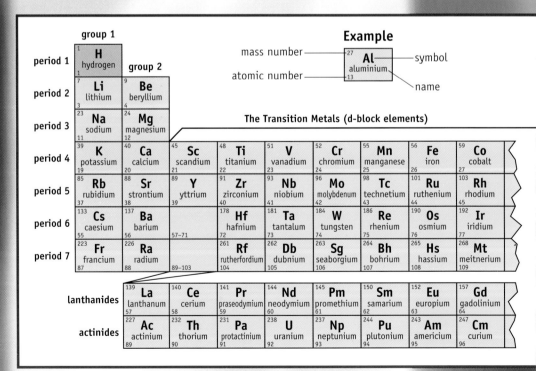

less reactive and their boiling points increase. At the top of the group, fluorine and chlorine are both gases at room temperature. Fluorine is the most reactive element of all and will even attack glass. Bromine, in the middle of the group, is the only non-metal element that is liquid at room temperature. Near the bottom of the group, iodine is a solid at room temperature and is much less reactive than the three elements positioned above it. The group 5 elements also have gradual changes as you proceed down their group, as you will see.

Nitrogen and group 5

There are five elements in group 5: nitrogen, phosphorus, arsenic, antimony and bismuth. These elements and their **compounds** are useful to us in many ways. In this book, you will discover lots of things about them and how they are used.

▼ *This is the periodic table of the elements. Group 5 contains nitrogen and phosphorus, which are non-metals; arsenic and antimony, which are metalloids; and bismuth, which is a metal.*

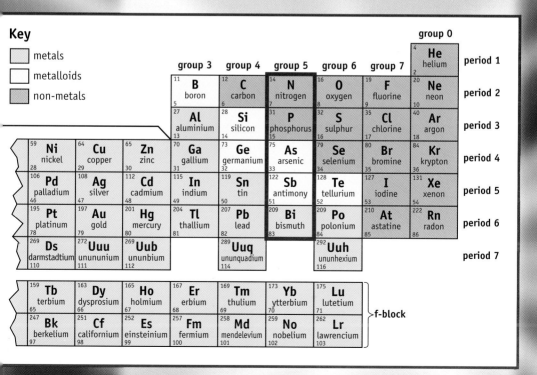

Elements of group 5

The **elements** in **group** 5 are all solids at room temperature, apart from nitrogen, which is a gas. Nitrogen and phosphorus are at the top of the group and are non-metals. Arsenic and antimony are in the middle of the group and are both metalloids. This means that they have some properties of non-metals and some of metals. Bismuth, at the bottom of the group, is a metal.

14	
N	**nitrogen**
nitrogen	*symbol: N • atomic number: 7 • non-metal*
7	

What does it look like? Nitrogen is a colourless gas with no smell or taste. It will normally only **react** with other elements when it is heated.

Where is it found? Nitrogen gas forms 78 per cent of the air we breathe and is combined with other elements in various **compounds**, such as saltpetre (potassium nitrate, KNO_3). Proteins, **DNA** and other complex compounds in living things also contain nitrogen.

What are its main uses? Nitrogen is often used to provide an unreactive atmosphere in oil tankers and during the manufacture of electronic devices. Liquid nitrogen is extremely cold, so it is used in medicine to freeze blood and other substances as well as the food industry to freeze food. The biggest single use for nitrogen is the manufacture of ammonia, NH_3. This has a huge number of uses that include making **fertilizers**, explosives, plastics and artificial fibres such as nylon.

Nitrogen is found in plastics and artificial fibres, such as the nylon climbing rope used by this rock climber. ▶

<table>
<tr><td>31
P
phosphorus
15</td><td>**phosphorus**
symbol: P • atomic number: 15 • non-metal</td></tr>
</table>

What does it look like?   Phosphorus is a solid element that exists in three different forms, called allotropes. White phosphorus glows in the dark and burns in air without needing to be heated first. If it is warmed carefully it becomes red phosphorus, which is less reactive than white phosphorus. Black phosphorus is the least reactive of the three forms. Like graphite (a form of carbon) it conducts electricity, which is very unusual for non-metals.

Where is it found?   Phosphorus does not exist naturally as a pure element because it is so reactive, but it is found in compounds. It often combines with oxygen to form compounds called phosphates. Like nitrogen, phosphorus is found in complex compounds in living things, such as DNA. Our bones and teeth contain phosphorus.

What are its main uses?   Phosphorus is used in matches and in bombs designed to set their targets on fire. Phosphorus compounds are widely used in fertilizers, detergents and toothpastes. Several phosphorus compounds are poisonous and are used to kill harmful insects.

Phosphorus is found in pesticides, which are chemicals used to kill insects and other pests that damage agricultural and horticultural crops, such as these ferns, which will be sold as pot plants.

More elements of group 5

75		arsenic
As		symbol: As • atomic number: 33 • metalloid
arsenic		
33		

What does it look like?   Arsenic, pronounced 'ars-nik', is a solid **element**. It has at least two different forms or allotropes, including yellow arsenic and grey arsenic. The most common form is grey arsenic, which consists of very brittle, metallic crystals. It burns in air to produce arsenic oxide, a solid with a smell similar to garlic. Arsenic is unusual because it sublimes when it is heated, which means that it turns directly from a solid into a gas without becoming a liquid in between.

Where is it found?   Although arsenic is sometimes found as the element itself, it is usually combined with other elements in various **compounds**. The **minerals** realgar (pronounced ree-al-gar) and orpiment contain arsenic sulphide. However, arsenic is normally produced from the wastes left over when copper and lead are **extracted** from their **ores**.

What are its main uses?   Arsenic is used in the manufacture of computer chips, while lead-arsenic **alloys** are important for producing car batteries and pellets for shot guns. Arsenic compounds are poisonous and are used to make wood preservatives.

122		antimony
Sb		symbol: Sb • atomic number: 51 • metalloid
antimony		
51		

What does it look like?   Antimony is a solid element that exists in different forms, including black antimony powder and yellow antimony crystals. The most common form consists of hard, brittle crystals with a blue-white colour. Antimony burns in air when it is heated, producing white fumes of antimony oxide.

Where is it found?   Antimony sometimes exists as a pure element. However, this is rare and it is usually found in various minerals, such as stibnite (antimony sulphide).

Like arsenic, antimony can be extracted from the wastes produced by **refining** copper or lead. The lead plates in car batteries often contain antimony and a lot of it is recycled from them.

What are its main uses?   Antimony is often mixed with metals to make alloys that are more hardwearing than the metal alone, such as the lead in car batteries. Antimony compounds make textiles and plastics more resistant to flames and they are used to colour pottery glazes and paint.

◀ *Even a fast sports car like this one needs a battery to start it up. The metal plates in car batteries are made from lead hardened with antimony.*

209 **Bi** bismuth 83	**bismuth**
	symbol: Bi • atomic number: 83 • metal

What does it look like?   Bismuth is a brittle, white metal, with a pink tint. When it is heated in air, it burns to form yellow bismuth oxide. Unlike most metals, bismuth is a poor conductor of heat and electricity.

Where is it found?   Bismuth is often found as a pure element, unlike the other solids in group 5. It also combines with other elements in various minerals, including bismite (bismuth oxide) and bismuthinite (bismuth sulphide). Most bismuth is extracted from the wastes produced from copper, lead, tin or silver refining.

What are its main uses?   Bismuth is mixed with other metals to make alloys with low melting points, which are used in electrical fuses and in automatic sprinkler systems that put out fires. Cosmetics such as lipstick may contain bismuth compounds to give them an attractive shine.

CHAPTER 3

Nitrogen

Nitrogen is colourless and has no smell or taste. If nitrogen is cooled to −196 °C or below, it condenses to form a clear liquid. Although nitrogen does not normally **react**, it will if it is heated with reactive metals such as magnesium to form metal nitrides.

> The word equation for magnesium reacting with nitrogen is:
>
> $$\text{magnesium} + \text{nitrogen} \xrightarrow{\text{heat}} \text{magnesium nitride}$$
>
> *Magnesium nitride is a yellow-green solid.*

Nitrogen also reacts with oxygen in the heat of a car engine, producing gases called nitrogen oxides or NOx. However it does not react readily with water and each litre of water at room temperature only contains about 16 cm^3 of dissolved nitrogen gas.

Foul, burnt, noxious air

During 1772 several chemists investigated air and managed to produce nitrogen from it. These included Carl Scheele, the Swedish chemist who discovered chlorine, and the English chemists Joseph Priestley (who discovered oxygen) and Henry Cavendish (who discovered hydrogen). Scheele called the gas 'foul air' because both living things and fire died in it. Cavendish named it burnt air because it was left over after burning charcoal. However, a Scottish chemist called Daniel Rutherford published his results first and was credited with the discovery of nitrogen, which he called noxious air. The word nitrogen comes from the Greek words meaning 'saltpetre-forming' (saltpetre is potassium nitrate, KNO_3).

Daniel Rutherford (1749–1815) discovered nitrogen in 1772. ▶

Nitrogen, the unliving gas

A French chemist called Antoine Lavoisier showed that nitrogen is an **element**, in 1776. Lavoisier called it '*azote*', after the Greek words meaning 'not living' because nitrogen is so unreactive. The French still call nitrogen *azote*.

Nitrogen everywhere

Nitrogen is an important component of the complex chemicals that make up living things, such as **DNA** and proteins. Although it is found in **minerals** such as saltpetre, it is easier to **extract** nitrogen from the atmosphere. Air is 78.08 per cent nitrogen and the atmosphere contains an amazing four thousand trillion tonnes of it!

Fractional distillation

When steam from a kettle of boiling water touches a cold surface, it cools and condenses back into liquid water. Similarly, when air is cooled down enough, the gases it contains **liquefy** or turn into liquids. Air is cooled to about −200 °C, so that most of the gases it contains are liquefied. If the mixture of liquids is allowed to warm up again slowly, each gas boils off at a different temperature. This is called **fractional distillation** of liquefied air. The nitrogen boils off first and is stored in pressurized containers. Other gases are collected as the liquefied air warms up, including oxygen and the noble gases argon, krypton and xenon.

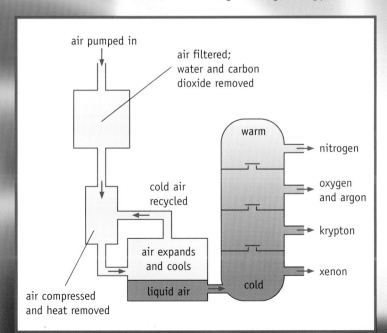

◀ *This diagram shows how air is separated into the different gases it contains by fractional distillation. As the liquefied air warms up, nitrogen boils off and is collected at the top of the fractionating column.*

air pumped in

air filtered; water and carbon dioxide removed

warm

nitrogen

cold air recycled

oxygen and argon

krypton

air expands and cools

xenon

cold

air compressed and heat removed

liquid air

Liquid nitrogen

Liquid nitrogen is a colourless liquid that boils at −196 °C. It is extremely cold and must be stored in special containers called Dewar flasks. These are very similar to **vacuum** flasks that are used to keep drinks hot or cold. Anyone using liquid nitrogen has to wear gloves and a face shield or safety glasses to protect them from splashes because it freezes things in seconds.

Dewar and the vacuum flask

Sir James Dewar, a Scottish scientist, invented a container for keeping hot liquids hot and cold liquids cold in 1892. The Dewar flask, also known as the vacuum or thermos flask, is really two glass containers, one inside the other. There is a vacuum between the two containers that stops heat moving in or out of the flask by conduction. The glass is coated in shiny metal to reduce the movement of heat by radiation.

Dewar flasks, also called vacuum flasks, keep coffee and other drinks hot in cold places. They also keep very cold liquids like liquid nitrogen cold in warm places.

Warts and all

Doctors use liquid nitrogen for cryosurgery, which is surgery using very cold tools. Warts and verrucas are small lumps that form on the skin. They often go away on their own eventually, but they are not attractive and can hurt if they are on the sole of a foot. To remove a wart or verruca, the doctor freezes it with some liquid nitrogen. The wart or verruca eventually falls off without any bleeding, although it can feel sore for a short while.

Liquid nitrogen is widely used to freeze scientific and medical samples, such as sensitive chemicals and blood. Dipping the tubes that contain the samples into liquid nitrogen freezes them very quickly. The tubes are stored in large Dewar flasks of liquid nitrogen so they remain extremely cold. Single cells and small amounts of tissue can be stored for a long time like this and continue to live after being thawed.

A scientist showing samples of cells stored in liquid nitrogen. Notice the thick protective gloves she is wearing to protect her hands from the intense cold.

However, it does not work for larger samples such as kidneys, because they become damaged when they are frozen. Organs intended for use in transplant operations are chilled and not frozen for this reason.

Freezing farm animals

You cannot freeze a whole cow and expect it to be alive after it has been thawed. However, sperm samples from bulls and other farm animals are often frozen and stored in liquid nitrogen. After thawing, the sperm begin to move again and can fertilize egg cells. This allows the farmers to breed more offspring from prize-winning animals.

Superconductors

Liquid nitrogen is used to keep superconducting magnets cold. Metals are good conductors of electricity, but at very low temperatures they can become superconductors. This means that they do not resist the flow of electricity at all. Electromagnets made from superconductors are extremely powerful and are used in magnetic resonance imaging (MRI) scanners, which doctors use to build up detailed images of the body.

Nitrogen gas

Nitrogen is very useful for preventing fires. When something is burning, it is **reacting** with the oxygen in air. If the oxygen is removed, the reaction has to stop and the fire goes out. If there is no oxygen there in the first place, a fire cannot start. Nitrogen gas is used to provide an unreactive atmosphere in oil tankers that reduces the risk of fire and explosions by keeping oxygen away from the fuel. The unreactive atmosphere provided by nitrogen gas is useful to us in other ways too.

Bonds, triple bonds

*Each nitrogen **molecule** is made from two nitrogen **atoms**. These are joined together by three chemical **bonds**. A lot of energy is needed to break these bonds, so nitrogen is quite unreactive.*

Keeping oxygen out

When steel is rolled or bent into shape, it can become brittle and difficult to work. If the steel is heated up and allowed to cool down again, it becomes easier to shape again. This is called annealing. However, hot steel will react with oxygen in the air. To stop this happening, annealing is usually carried out in a mixture of nitrogen and hydrogen, which keeps oxygen away from the metal. Nitrogen is used in a similar way to prevent electronic components from reacting with oxygen while they are being made.

Don't let mould spoil your dinner

Some fungi are useful to us because we eat them. Fungi such as mushrooms are a good source of protein and fungi produce the fine lines in blue cheeses, like Stilton. In addition, food scientists have been able to use some types of fungi to make tasty alternatives to meat for vegetarians. However, other types of fungi are not so useful because they make our food go mouldy. Food also goes bad if bacteria grow on it and if the nutrients in the food react with oxygen in the air. If oxygen is kept away from the food, fungi and bacteria cannot grow on it so easily and the chemical reactions that spoil it are prevented. Therefore food manufacturers often package food in a protective atmosphere of nitrogen and carbon dioxide. They may also use liquid nitrogen to preserve food by chilling or freezing it.

▲
This bread has the fungus Penicillium *growing on it. The white areas are part of a network of tiny filaments called hyphae that grow into the bread and digest it, while the blue areas are spores that can spread the fungus to other food. Packaging bread in an atmosphere of nitrogen and carbon dioxide keeps oxygen away and fungi cannot grow on it so easily.*

Fire-fighting foam

There are many different types of fire extinguishers, including those that smother flames with foam, water or dry powder. These extinguishers need a gas called a **propellant** to shoot the contents out of the extinguisher. Nitrogen is used as a propellant because it is not flammable and will not make the fire worse. However, nitrogen is rarely used in aerosol cans because it escapes each time the contents are sprayed out. The pressure gradually goes down and the aerosol becomes less and less effective. For this reason most aerosol cans use liquefied gases such as propane and butane for their propellant, although these gases are flammable and cannot be used for aerosols that contain food.

Ammonia and the Haber process

The main use of nitrogen is in the manufacture of ammonia, NH_3, which is a colourless gas with a sharp, choking smell. Ammonia has a huge range of uses, including making **fertilizers**, explosives and plastics. Over a hundred million tonnes of it are manufactured around the world each year.

The Haber process

Ammonia is manufactured using the Haber process. Fritz Haber took four years to develop his process and was awarded the Nobel Prize for Chemistry in 1918 for his work. The raw materials for the Haber process are natural gas, air and water. These are used to make nitrogen and hydrogen, which are forced to **react** together to make ammonia.

This is Fritz Haber (1868–1934), the German chemist who developed a way to make ammonia from nitrogen and hydrogen, heated under pressure with an iron catalyst.

Nitrogen and hydrogen

*Natural gas **reacts** with steam, producing carbon dioxide and hydrogen. The carbon dioxide is removed, purified and sold to make the bubbles in fizzy drinks. Some of the hydrogen is used to make ammonia, while the rest is burned in air. In this reaction, the hydrogen reacts with oxygen in the air to make more steam, which is then cooled and condensed to form water. This has the effect of removing the oxygen from the air, leaving nitrogen behind ready to react with the hydrogen.*

Nitrogen and hydrogen are reacted together by putting them under high pressure, typically two hundred times atmospheric pressure. The rate of the reaction is increased using lumps of iron as a **catalyst** and by raising the temperature to about 450 °C. Even under these conditions only about fifteen per cent of the gases react together. The mixture of nitrogen, hydrogen and ammonia is cooled and the ammonia condenses to form a liquid that is piped off. The unreacted nitrogen and hydrogen are recycled and the process repeated.

The word equation for the Haber process is:

$$nitrogen + hydrogen \rightleftharpoons ammonia$$

Most reactions you see at school go to completion and cannot be reversed. This one is reversible, however, so we use the $\rightleftharpoons$ symbol instead of the usual arrow.

A difficult problem

Most of the ammonia produced is used to make artificial fertilizers. Without them, farmers could not grow enough food for everyone. At the start of the 20th century, nitrogen fertilizers were made from Chile saltpetre (sodium nitrate, $NaNO_3$), but demand was outstripping supply. When Haber developed his process in 1909, the world no longer depended upon a limited supply of Chile saltpetre and farmyard manure. Unfortunately, ammonia can also be used to make explosives. When World War I broke out in 1914, the Haber process allowed the Germans to continue manufacturing explosives, despite the Allies blocking the transport of Chile saltpetre to Germany. This prolonged the war and contributed to the vast number of casualties, which included over eight million dead.

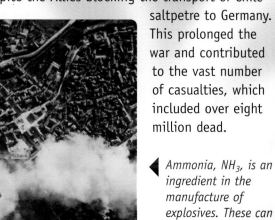

◀ *Ammonia, NH_3, is an ingredient in the manufacture of explosives. These can be used by miners, demolition experts and for making bombs such as these.*

Uses of ammonia

Around 80 per cent of the ammonia produced is used to make **fertilizers**. It can be drilled directly into the soil as it is easily **liquefied** by putting it under pressure or by cooling it below −33 °C. Hardly any ammonia escapes back out of the soil as it dissolves easily in the soil's water.

This experiment is often called the ammonia fountain. The top flask contains ammonia, which dissolves very easily in water. As the ammonia dissolves, the pressure in the flask is reduced. This forces more water up from the bottom flask making a fountain. The water contains universal indicator, which turns purple because the ammonia solution is alkaline.

Cleaning up with ammonia

A colourless **alkaline** solution, sometimes called ammonium hydroxide solution, is made when ammonia dissolves in water. Even though it is smelly, this is used in some household cleaners. Alkalis **react** with oil and grease, breaking them down so they are easier to remove from kitchen worktops and bathroom fittings. You should wear rubber gloves when using ammonium hydroxide solution because, like other alkalis, ammonia is corrosive and damages skin.

Fridges and freezers

Fridges and freezers work by removing heat from the inside of the machine and depositing it outside. A refrigerant is pumped through pipes inside and outside the fridge. Refrigerants are liquids that easily evaporate to form a gas and condense to form a liquid again. Ammonia does this well and is used as the refrigerant in many fridges and freezers especially industrial and commercial machines.

What's in your fridge?

The liquid refrigerant is forced through a tiny hole inside the pipes, causing it to turn into a very cold gas and this chills the air inside the fridge. The cold refrigerant gas is then pumped to a compressor, which puts it under pressure so that it heats up. The heat is transferred into the room through pipes at the back of the fridge and the refrigerant becomes a liquid to start the cycle again.

Smelling salts

If you have changed a baby's nappy or cleaned a pet's cage, you will know the smell of ammonia, because it is produced when urine goes off. Ammonia irritates the nose and lungs and can trigger a reflex that causes us to breathe faster. Ammonium carbonate is a white solid that easily breaks down to release ammonia fumes and is used in smelling salts. These are used to wake up people who have fainted.

▲
Ammonia is produced when urine goes stale. You can often smell ammonia when you clean your pet's cage.

Hardening steel

Steel machinery components are made more hardwearing by a process called nitriding. The component is put into an atmosphere containing ammonia gas. This is heated to 500 °C; the ammonia breaks down to form nitrogen and hydrogen atoms; over several days, the nitrogen atoms fill microscopic spaces in the surface of the steel, making it much tougher.

Ammonia and nitric acid

Around five per cent of ammonia is converted into nitric acid. This is a very useful substance and about 60 million tonnes of nitric acid are made in the world each year.

Making nitric acid

Nitric acid, HNO_3, is a very strong acid. It can be made in the laboratory by heating a mixture of potassium nitrate, KNO_3, and sulphuric acid. However, it is made on an industrial scale from ammonia, air and water by the Ostwald process. Wilhelm Ostwald, a German chemist, patented this process in 1902. He was awarded the 1909 Nobel Prize for Chemistry in recognition of his work on rates of chemical **reactions**.

The Ostwald process

In the first step of the Ostwald process, ammonia and air are passed over a heated platinum-rhodium **catalyst**. *This produces nitrogen monoxide gas, NO, and steam:*

ammonia + oxygen → nitrogen monoxide + steam

The nitrogen monoxide then reacts with more oxygen from the air to produce nitrogen dioxide gas, NO_2:

nitrogen monoxide + oxygen → nitrogen dioxide

Nitric acid is formed when nitrogen dioxide, oxygen from the air, and water react together:

nitrogen dioxide + oxygen + water → nitric acid

Ammonium nitrate

Ammonia dissolves in water to form ammonium hydroxide, which is alkaline. When this is mixed with nitric acid, the two chemicals react to produce a white solid called ammonium nitrate, which accounts for 80 per cent of the nitric acid produced.

The word equation for producing ammonium nitrate is:

ammonium
hydroxide + nitric acid → ammonium nitrate + water

This is a **neutralization** reaction, where an alkali and an acid react together to produce a salt and water.

Farmers use ammonium nitrate pellets or 'nitram' as an artificial **fertilizer**. It is a very good source of nitrogen and plants can take ammonium nitrate up through their roots easily because it dissolves in water. Similar **compounds** are used in other fertilizers, such as ammonium sulphate and ammonium phosphate.

Most ammonium nitrate is used to manufacture fertilizers, but explosives are also made from it. Ammonium nitrate breaks down when it is heated or moved vigorously enough. If this happens in a container it can explode. In 1947, a cargo ship carrying ammonium nitrate fertilizer caught fire and exploded in Texas City harbour, Texas, USA. Two more ships and a chemical factory were destroyed, killing nearly six hundred people. Ammonium nitrate is usually mixed with other chemicals, such as fuel oil, to produce commercial explosives for mining and demolition work.

◀ *Ammonium nitrate decomposes above 210 ºC to produce poisonous fumes. It is an* **oxidizing agent** *that causes other substances to burn very vigorously and it can explode.*

Nitric acid, dyes and plastics

Although nitric acid is mostly used to produce ammonium nitrate, it is also an important ingredient in the manufacturing of dyes and plastics.

Nitric acid and metals

Unreactive metals, such as copper, do not usually **react** with acids, but nitric acid is an exception. Nitric acid is used to etch copper and brass to make attractive pictures and for 'pickling' metals. When metals are rolled into shape, they become coated in a layer of metal oxides, especially if the metals are hot. Pickling involves removing these oxides with an acid to leave a shiny surface behind. Other chemicals are often mixed with nitric acid when it is used for pickling, otherwise it eats away the metal too.

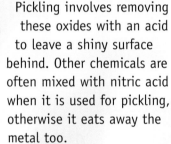

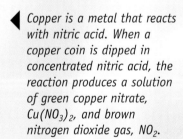

◀ Copper is a metal that reacts with nitric acid. When a copper coin is dipped in concentrated nitric acid, the reaction produces a solution of green copper nitrate, $Cu(NO_3)_2$, and brown nitrogen dioxide gas, NO_2.

Royal water

Gold stays shiny because it does not react with air or water. Usually it does not react with acids either. However, a mixture of concentrated nitric acid and hydrochloric acid will actually dissolve gold! This mixture of acids is called *aqua regia*, which means 'royal water' because it dissolves unreactive or noble metals. *Aqua regia* is used widely by the metals industry to separate gold from other precious metals, such as rhodium.

Dyes and plastics

Nitric acid is very important in the chemical industry for the manufacture of dyes and plastics, such as nylon and the stretchy artificial fibres used in sports clothing. These materials do not contain nitric acid itself, but it is used to produce chemicals called intermediates that react further to make the final **product**. For example, nitric acid is used to make dinitrotoluene (pronounced di-nitro-toll-you-een) or DNT for short. DNT in turn is required to make polyurethane foams for stuffing furniture. You may not have heard of DNT before, but you are likely to have heard about a related chemical called trinitrotoluene (pronounced try-nitro-toll-you-een) otherwise known as TNT.

Nitric acid is used in the manufacture of the stretchy, artificial fibres used in sports clothing worn here by the US gymnastics team.

TNT is a yellow solid that is made using nitric acid. It is widely used as an explosive for demolishing old buildings. It is safe for the demolition experts to use because it needs a **detonator** to make it explode. Nitric acid is also used to make other explosives, such as nitroglycerine.

Mauve – the first artificial dye

The very first artificial dye was not made by a large team of research chemists, but by William Perkin in 1856 when he was just eighteen years old! While doing some chemical experiments at home, Perkin accidentally made a purple dye from phenylamine, which is a chemical made with nitric acid. He started a family business to make and sell the dye, known as mauve, and became very wealthy.

Explosives and other nitrogen compounds

Gunpowder is an explosive mixture of carbon, sulphur and potassium nitrate, discovered by the Chinese over a thousand years ago. It was not until the middle of the nineteenth century that experiments with nitric acid led to the discovery of new explosives.

Nitroglycerine and dynamite

Ascanio Sobrero, an Italian chemist, discovered nitroglycerine in 1846. It is a colourless liquid, made by **reacting** nitric acid with a type of alcohol called glycerol. The reaction itself is very dangerous and nitroglycerine can explode just by being knocked. In 1865, a Swedish chemist called Alfred Nobel began making nitroglycerine on an industrial scale. Tragically, an explosion at his factory killed five people, including his brother. A year later, he discovered that nitroglycerine becomes safer to handle when it is mixed with absorbent material. Nobel called his discovery 'dynamite' and it made him rich.

This is a portrait of Alfred Nobel (1833–1896), the Swedish chemist who invented dynamite in 1866 and set up the famous Nobel Prizes.

The Nobel Prizes

Alfred Nobel died in 1896 and left a large part of his fortune in his will to fund some very special awards. Each year since 1900, the Nobel Foundation has awarded Nobel Prizes to men and women who have made outstanding contributions to Physics, Chemistry, Medicine, Literature or Peace.

A pain in the chest

If the coronary arteries that provide blood to the heart get narrower because of disease, the heart cells do not get enough blood. This causes a sharp chest pain called angina. Nitroglycerine tablets, skin patches or sprays relax the coronary arteries. This makes them wider, increasing the flow of blood again and easing the pain. Butyl nitrate and amyl nitrate do a similar job.

Beware of the NOx

Car engines need an air supply to burn fuel. Unfortunately nitrogen and oxygen in the air react together in a hot car engine to make nitrogen oxides. These are usually just called NOx because the numbers of nitrogen and oxygen **atoms** in the **molecules** vary. If these gases escape into the atmosphere, they dissolve in the clouds, making nitrous acid and nitric acid. These cause acid rain, which damages living things and buildings. Catalytic converters, fitted to modern cars, change NOx gases into harmless nitrogen.

Laughing gas

Nitrous oxide, N_2O, is an anaesthetic gas used by some dentists to put their patients to sleep before removing teeth. It is also called laughing gas because in smaller doses it causes people to behave in a silly way. Nitrous oxide is a **propellant** in aerosols and boosts racing car engines. It breaks down in the heat of the car engine, providing extra oxygen to make the car go faster.

Nitrous oxide, N_2O, provides the pressure needed to squirt cream from aerosol cans.

Nitrogen in living things

Living things produce very large and complex **molecules** by joining lots of small molecules together. Many of these molecules, like **deoxyribonucleic acid (DNA)** and proteins, contain nitrogen. DNA provides the information needed to make different proteins in cells. A single molecule of human DNA can be 7 cm long, but it is tightly curled up into spirals so that it fits into the nucleus of the cell.

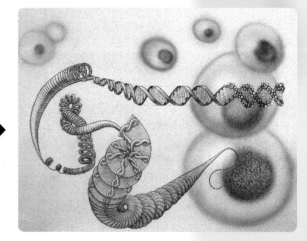

*DNA is the molecule that holds the genetic information in our cells. It contains nitrogen, phosphorus and three other **elements**: carbon, oxygen and hydrogen. DNA has to be coiled in several ways to fit into the cell's nucleus.*

Amines

An ammonia molecule is made from one nitrogen **atom** and three hydrogen atoms, joined together by chemical **bonds**. If one or more of the hydrogen atoms are replaced by a chain or ring of carbon atoms, we get molecules called amines. Although small amines smell like ammonia, big ones smell fishy (fish proteins break down to form amines). Amines can be made artificially and are very useful. For example, ethylamine, $C_2H_5NH_2$, is used in the manufacture of rubber, pesticides and dyes.

Amino acids and proteins

Amino acids are small molecules that join together to make large molecules called polypeptides or even larger molecules called proteins. Amino acids are joined end to end by single nitrogen atoms, like a bridge. These are called peptide bonds. When we digest proteins from our food, enzymes produced by the stomach and small intestine break peptide bonds, releasing amino acids.

Protein in our diet

Proteins are the main source of nitrogen in our diet. Foods such as meat, fish, dairy products and beans are rich in protein.

Urine, urea and uric acid

When proteins in our bodies break down into amino acids, the liver converts them into a chemical called urea, H_2NCONH_2. Urea is transported in our bloodstream to the kidneys, where it is removed from the blood. The urea dissolves in water and passes out of our bodies as urine. Birds and reptiles are slightly different and produce very concentrated uric acid, $C_5H_4N_4O_3$. The uric acid from bird droppings reacts with limestone and metals used in many buildings and damages car paintwork.

Urea as a fertilizer

Urea is made industrially from ammonia and carbon dioxide. It is used as a **fertilizer** to replace nitrogen in the soil. It gradually breaks down to release ammonia that plants can use.

Gout

The liver converts amino acids into uric acid, as well as urea, which is also removed by the kidneys. If this does not happen properly or too much uric acid is made, we get gout. This is a painful disease caused by crystals of uric acid building up in the body. The crystals can produce little white pimples under the skin and make the joints swollen and painful. The big toe is usually the first joint to be affected, but gout can also attack other joints such as the wrist, knee or elbow.

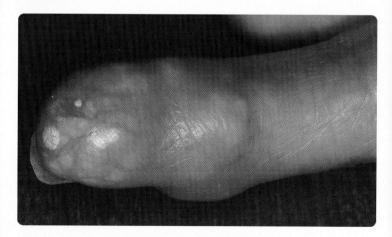

▲
This is the finger of someone suffering from gout. You can see white skin pimples and a swollen joint caused by crystals of uric acid that build up in the body.

The nitrogen cycle

Nitrogen is an important **element** for living things, as it is found in proteins and other **molecules**. Although the atmosphere contains a huge amount of nitrogen gas, most living things cannot use it. Plants can only absorb nitrogen as nitrates through their roots and animals have to eat the proteins in plants and other animals. The different processes involved are linked together in the nitrogen cycle.

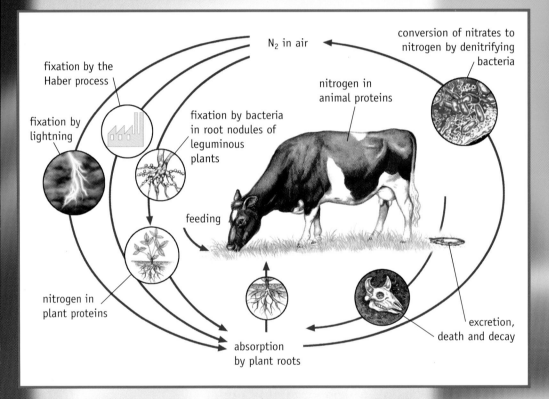

This diagram shows the main processes in the nitrogen cycle. Nitrogen from the air is converted into ammonia, nitrates and proteins. It is eventually returned to the atmosphere by denitrifying bacteria.

That'll fix it

When nitrogen gas is converted into **compounds** it is called nitrogen fixation. Lightning causes nitrogen and oxygen to **react** together to produce nitrogen oxides or NOx. NOx dissolves in the clouds, producing nitrous acid and nitric acid, which gets into the soil when it rains. Around ten million tonnes of nitrogen are fixed like this each year. However twice as much nitrogen is fixed when fuels are burned. In the heat of an engine or furnace, nitrogen and oxygen again react together to produce NOx.

The Haber process produces ammonia by reacting nitrogen and hydrogen together, fixing over eighty million tonnes of nitrogen each year.

Busy bacteria

Nitrogen-fixing bacteria live in the soil and sometimes in plant roots. They absorb nitrogen from the atmosphere and use it to make nitrogen compounds such as ammonia. Nitrifying bacteria convert ammonia into nitrates. Bacteria fix about 175 million tonnes of nitrogen each year.

A special relationship

Some nitrogen-fixing bacteria live in plant roots. A plant group called the legumes, which includes peas, beans and clover, are well known for this. The bacteria live inside swellings on the roots, called nodules, and are provided with food, while the plants get nitrates. This is called a symbiotic relationship.

Back to the start

Denitrifying bacteria in the soil use nitrates as food and break them down to form nitrogen gas, which then escapes back into the atmosphere.

Using nitrogen compounds

Green plants absorb nitrates from the soil through their roots or from bacteria in their root nodules. The plants use these nitrates to make proteins, such as green chlorophyll. When animals eat plants, the amino acids that make up the plant proteins are used to make animal proteins, such as muscle. Fungi and bacteria break down the animal waste and proteins from dead plants and animals to form ammonia and similar compounds. Nitrifying bacteria convert these back into nitrates, ready for plants to absorb, starting the cycle again.

Phosphorus

Phosphorus is a very **reactive**, solid **element**. It has three different forms, called allotropes. White phosphorus is the most reactive and must be kept under water because it bursts into flames when it is exposed to air. The reaction produces a brilliant white light and clouds of white phosphorus pentoxide, P_2O_5. If white phosphorus is heated very gently it becomes the less reactive allotrope, red phosphorus. Black phosphorus is the least reactive of the three forms and conducts electricity, even though it is a non-metal.

Phosphorus was discovered in 1669. It is a very reactive non-metal that has to be stored under water to stop it igniting in air. ▶

Don't try this at home

A German called Hennig Brand discovered and isolated phosphorus in 1669. He was interested in alchemy, a medieval form of chemistry, in which alchemists tried to turn metals such as lead into gold or silver. Like many alchemists, Brand wondered if the colour of urine meant that it contained gold. He collected over fifty buckets of urine and evaporated most of the water. He left the remains for about two weeks, by which time worms were living in it! Brand distilled this foul material and produced a waxy solid. He called it phosphorus after the Greek words meaning 'light bearer' as it glowed in the dark. In 1777, the French chemist Antoine Lavoisier showed that phosphorus was an element.

Brand's chemistry

Urine contains water, salts and **compounds** from the breakdown of proteins and other complex chemicals. When these are heated, the compounds that contain phosphorus react with other compounds and the phosphorus is released. Phosphorus has a low boiling point, so it is easily separated from the rest of the material by **distillation**. However, it reacts immediately with oxygen in the air, so it has to be collected under water.

Finding phosphorus

Phosphorus is found combined with oxygen and other elements in various **minerals**, generally called phosphate rock. Apatite or calcium phosphate, $Ca_3(PO_4)_2$, is the most important type. Over 130 million tonnes of phosphate rock are mined in the world each year, mainly in the USA, North Africa and China.

◀ *The pale pink mineral in this mixture of crystals is apatite – calcium phosphate.*

Phosphorus is usually extracted from phosphate rock by heating it to about 1500 °C with sand and coke, which is a cheap form of nearly pure carbon. The reaction produces carbon monoxide gas and a molten slag containing calcium silicate and other by-products. Phosphorus boils at only 280 °C and escapes from the reaction mixture as a gas. It is then solidified by cooling and stored under water. Very little of the phosphorus is used on its own – most of it is converted into compounds containing phosphorus.

The word equation for the extraction of phosphorus from calcium phosphate rock is:

calcium phosphate + silicon dioxide + carbon → calcium silicate + carbon monoxide + phosphorus

Sand is mostly silica or silicon dioxide and the carbon comes from coke.

Uses of phosphorus

Although steel that contains phosphorus is much harder, it is brittle and more likely to crack. Modern steel usually contains only very small amounts of phosphorus and sometimes it is viewed as an impurity. However, phosphorus is often added deliberately to other metals to improve their properties.

Titanic and phosphorus

The *Titanic* was a passenger liner that sank on 12 April 1912 after hitting an iceberg. Around 1500 people died. The *Titanic* was supposed to be unsinkable, but she sank in less than three hours. Analyses of steel samples brought back to the surface from the *Titanic* showed her steel contained more phosphorus and other **elements** than would be allowed today, making it much weaker than modern steel.

Phosphor bronze

Bronze is an **alloy** of copper with small amounts of tin. If phosphorus is added too, it makes phosphor bronze, which is harder than bronze alone. Only very small amounts of phosphorus are needed and a typical phosphor bronze may contain 94.8 per cent copper and 5 per cent tin, with just 0.2 per cent phosphorus. Phosphor bronze can be cast into machinery parts, including springs, gears and valves that need to be strong.

▼ *The RMS* Titanic *was a luxury liner that was supposed to be unsinkable. Tragically, it sank on its first voyage in 1912 after hitting an iceberg on the journey from Southampton to New York.*

Smoke screens and bombs

White phosphorus immediately **reacts** with oxygen when it is exposed to air, giving off white clouds of phosphorus pentoxide. This means it is useful for making smoke bombs and grenades. When the bomb explodes, clouds of white smoke make it difficult for the enemy to see where to aim. Phosphorus is also used in incendiary bombs, which are designed to set fire to buildings and equipment, rather than blowing them apart. A typical incendiary bomb contains phosphorus and oil in a glass container. When the bomb lands, its contents scatter everywhere and the phosphorus ignites, lighting the oil.

◀ *Phosphorus is used in smoke bombs, like this one used during an army training exercise. The smoke is thick enough to hide troops in a military vehicle from view.*

Matches

Red phosphorus is used to light safety matches (the sort that only light if scraped along the edge of the box). The match's head contains sulphur, potassium chlorate, $KClO_3$ and powdered glass to increase the friction when the match is struck. The edge of the box contains red phosphorus and powdered glass. The friction from striking the match produces enough heat to turn some of the red phosphorus into white phosphorus. This immediately catches fire, causing the potassium chlorate to break down. The oxygen released helps the sulphur to burn, which in turn sets fire to the matchstick.

Not as safe – any rough surface will do

Ordinary matches work differently. Their heads contain a mixture of phosphorus sulphide, P_4S_3, potassium chlorate and powdered glass. When the match is struck against a rough surface, enough heat is generated to ignite the phosphorus sulphide.

Phosphoric acid and phosphates

Most phosphorus is used in **compounds**; especially phosphoric acid and the phosphates made from it. Phosphoric acid, H_3PO_4, is made by **reacting** phosphate rock with sulphuric acid.

The word equation for the manufacture of phosphoric acid from phosphate rock (calcium phosphate) is:

calcium phosphate + sulphuric acid $\rightarrow$ calcium sulphate + phosphoric acid

Steel and cola

Phosphoric acid is used to clean and rust-proof steel. When steel rusts, the iron in it reacts with water and air to make a form of iron oxide, Fe_2O_3. Phosphoric acid reacts with iron oxide to produce a layer of iron phosphate, $FePO_4$, that keeps water and air away from the steel underneath.

Like all acids, phosphoric acid has a sharp taste, and it is used to flavour cola drinks. Although it is very dilute, it can still damage your teeth if you forget to brush them after drinking cola. Phosphoric acid is used to flavour other foods too, such as cheese and jam.

Fertilizers

Phosphorus is an important **mineral** for plants. Without it, their leaves become stunted and turn purple. Plant roots can only absorb minerals if they are dissolved in water, so **fertilizer** manufacturers make ammonium phosphate, $(NH_4)_3PO_4$, which is water-soluble. It is made by reacting ammonia with phosphoric acid. Ammonium phosphate is a useful fertilizer because it supplies plants with nitrogen as well as phosphorus.

This might look like a smooth lawn (opposite) but it's really a pond covered with tiny plants called algae. Phosphates and nitrates from waste water that contains detergents or fertilizers runs off the land into the pond. They cause the algae to grow very quickly. This kills fish because oxygen in the water is used up when the algae rot. ▶

The word equation for making ammonium phosphate is:

ammonia + phosphoric acid → ammonium phosphate

*This is a **neutralization** reaction between an alkali and an acid to make a salt.*

Detergents

Hard water contains dissolved calcium and magnesium compounds. These make it difficult to lather soap and they react with it to make a sticky grey-white scum. If the water is hard, you need more detergent and higher temperatures to get clothes clean. Manufacturers add 'water softener' to the detergents. These react with the calcium and magnesium in the water, surround them and stop them reacting with the detergent. Sodium tripolyphosphate (pronounced 'try-polly-foss-fate'), $Na_5P_3O_{10}$, is commonly added to detergents as a water softener.

Too much of a good thing?

Phosphates can get into lakes and streams from waste water containing detergents or from phosphate fertilizers and cause big problems. Water plants grow very quickly and can soon block a lake or stream. When the plants die and rot, a lot of oxygen in the water is used up. Fish and other animals in the water die because of lack of oxygen.

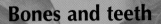

Bones and teeth

The skeleton, which is made from bone, supports the body and gives it a shape. It also allows the muscles to move the body and protects vital organs, such as the lungs and brain. There are about 700 g of phosphorus in a typical 65-kg person and about 80 per cent of this is stored in the bones and teeth.

Calcium phosphate

Bones need to be strong enough to carry the weight of a body, so they contain crystals of a hard **mineral** called hydroxylapatite. This type of calcium phosphate, $Ca_3(PO_4)_2$ accounts for over half the weight of bone. Bones also contain a tough elastic protein called collagen. This makes them slightly flexible so they do not snap easily when they are stretched or bent.

Our bones contain a hard mineral called hydroxylapatite, which is a type of calcium phosphate. About 80 per cent of the phosphorus in our body is stored in our bones and teeth. ▶

A composite material

Bones are made from a composite material because they contain both collagen and hydroxylapatite. Collagen is strong when stretched or bent, but easily squashed, while hydroxylapatite withstands being crushed, but is quite brittle.

Changing bones

Minerals naturally move in and out of bones, depending on our diet and how we use our bodies. Cells in bone called osteoblasts make hydroxylapatite, while other cells called osteoclasts break it down. This means that our bones are always changing, even though their overall shape stays the same. Bone builds up where more hydroxylapatite is produced than is removed and this usually happens when bone is put under pressure from exercise. Conversely, bone becomes weaker when it is not put under pressure, through lack of exercise. It is natural for bone to change like this throughout our life.

Phosphorus in our diet

Phosphorus is an important mineral in our diet. It is involved in releasing energy in our cells, making complex **molecules** such as **DNA** and for healthy bones and teeth. We, in the West, are very unlikely to suffer from phosphorus deficiency because a normal diet provides plenty of it. Foods such as cheese, eggs, bread and meat are all excellent sources of phosphorus.

If our diet contains too much phosphorus, calcium is released from the bones to help remove it from the body. This is not a problem unless there is is too little calcium in the diet. If this occurs the bones can become brittle and the joints painful. Foods such as milk and cheese are good sources of calcium.

Vitamin D

Vitamin D is important for controlling the levels of phosphorus and calcium in the body. Our bodies can make vitamin D when we are in sunshine. Margarine, butter and eggs are good sources of it too.

◀ *This omelette is made from eggs, which are a good source of phosphorus in our diet.*

Phosphorus in living things

Phosphorus is vital for many complex **molecules** in living things, apart from bones and teeth.

Pass the phosphorus

Our cells release energy from glucose, using a chemical **reaction** called respiration. Just over half of the energy in glucose is released as heat. The rest is used to convert a chemical called adenosine diphosphate (ADP) into adenosine triphosphate (ATP).

The word equation for respiration is:

glucose + oxygen $\rightarrow$ carbon dioxide + water

Respiration happens in mitochondria, which are tiny units that exist within every cell. The energy released by each molecule of glucose produces thirty-eight molecules of ATP.

Delivering energy

*ATP is a complex molecule, containing three 'phosphate groups' joined together in a line, that stores energy. If the last phosphate group in the line is removed by breaking a chemical **bond**, the ATP molecule becomes a molecule of ADP again. When this happens, energy is released for the cell to use. ATP delivers energy right where the cell needs it.*

DNA

Deoxyribonucleic acid (DNA) contains the cell's genetic information. DNA is made from many smaller molecules called nucleotides. These are joined end to end, using phosphate groups, to make a very big molecule.

The diagram (opposite) shows a cross-section through the membrane of an animal cell. Membranes control the movement of substances into and out of the cell. They contain proteins and two layers of phospholipid molecules, a type of fat that contains phosphorus. ▶

Fatty phosphorus

Although oils do not mix with water, some natural fats, called phospholipids (pronounced 'foss-fo-li-pids'), do dissolve very slightly in water. Phospholipids work in the body like detergents. The liver produces a yellow-green liquid called bile, which contains a type of phospholipid called phosphatidyl choline (pronounced fos-fa-ti-dile co-leen). Phosphatidyl choline surrounds fat and oil from our food, breaking them down into smaller droplets. This makes it easier for the enzymes to digest fat because they have a bigger surface area to work on.

◀ Lecithin, a **compound** containing phosphorus, is used in the manufacture of chocolates and cakes. It comes from vegetables and helps the ingredients mix properly.

Fatty food

Phosphatidyl choline is also called lecithin (pronounced 'lessy-thin'). Lecithin from vegetables, often mixed with other phospholipids, is widely used to help ingredients mix together better. It is found in products such as soap and cosmetics, and in foods such as chocolate and cakes.

Phosphates and fats form barriers

Like all fats and oils, phospholipids have a long 'tail' of carbon **atoms** that stops them dissolving, but they also have a 'head' containing a phosphate group that makes them dissolve. Phospholipids form a double layer in water, called a bilayer. This is a sheet of phospholipids with all the tails on the inside and all the heads on the outside. Cell membranes are made from phospholipid bilayers, with proteins to help keep them in shape. Fatty membranes are important for all cells, but especially for nerve cells. Phospholipids make up half of the dry weight of a brain.

CHAPTER 5

Arsenic

Arsenic is a poisonous solid and like phosphorus, has different forms or allotropes. Grey arsenic is the most common allotrope, which consists of brittle, metallic crystals, but arsenic also exists as yellow crystals. Arsenic does not **react** with water, but when heated in oxygen it burns to produce white arsenic pentoxide, As_2O_5. When heated, arsenic sublimes into a gas, without becoming a liquid first. Solid arsenic has to be heated under pressure to obtain the liquid.

The red parts on this piece of rock are made from realgar, a type of arsenic sulphide that has the chemical formula AsS.

Just sublime

When solids are heated, they usually melt into liquids, which then boil to become gases. When gases are cooled, they normally condense to form liquids, which freeze to form solids. However, some substances change directly from a solid to gas when heated and from a gas to a solid when cooled, without becoming a liquid at all. This change of state is called subliming. Dry ice, which is frozen carbon dioxide, sublimes to form a white vapour that is often used to give spooky effects in movies. Frozen food can be freeze-dried because ice sublimes if the air pressure is very low.

Ancient arsenic

The ancient Romans used arsenic **compounds** as medicines and the Victorians were still using them in the nineteenth century. However, people often had more sinister reasons for knowing about arsenic compounds – they are poisonous and have caused many suspicious deaths over the centuries.

In 1250, a German alchemist called Albertus Magnus **extracted** arsenic from orpiment (arsenic sulphide, As_2S_3) by heating it with soap. Although he was the first European to manage this, the ancient Chinese had worked out how to do it nearly a thousand years earlier. The name arsenic comes from the Greek word for orpiment.

◀ *These yellow crystals are orpiment, which is soft and heavy. Orpiment is a source of arsenic.*

Unearthing arsenic

Arsenic can be found as a pure **element**, although it is more often combined with sulphur to form arsenic sulphides, such as orpiment and realgar. The most common arsenic **mineral** is arsenopyrite or iron arsenic sulphide, FeAsS. If this is heated to about 700 °C, it breaks down to produce arsenic gas. When this is separated and cooled, it sublimes to form solid arsenic.

The word equation for the production of arsenic from arsenopyrite is:

$$\text{iron arsenic sulphide} \xrightarrow{\text{700 °C}} \text{iron sulphide + arsenic}$$

Copper and lead **ores** often contain arsenic compounds and a lot of arsenic is recovered from the wastes that remain after these metals have been extracted. Nearly half of the thirty-five thousand tonnes of arsenic produced in the world each year comes from China. Most of this is used in various arsenic compounds, rather than as a pure element.

Arsenic and chips

Arsenic is mixed with lead to produce an **alloy** used in ammunition, such as shotgun pellets. 'Drop shot' is made by pouring molten lead into a container at the top of a tall tower. The container is like a sieve and droplets of the molten lead fall through them. They solidify as they fall and are collected in water at the bottom. A small amount of arsenic, usually less than one per cent, is added to the lead to make the pellets more spherical. An English plumber called William Watts invented this method in 1783, even converting his house into a tall tower to start making lead pellets!

Falling through the air

*Drawings of water droplets falling through the air often show them as pear-shaped 'tear drops'. Surface tension causes water **molecules** at the surface of the drop to attract each other very strongly, and makes small droplets spherical. Arsenic increases the surface tension of lead, making the molten lead droplets rounder as they fall.*

When small drops of water fall through the air, surface tension pulls them into a round shape. Shotgun pellets are made from droplets of molten lead that contains arsenic. The arsenic makes the lead droplets rounder by increasing their surface tension.

Arsenic in semiconductors

Electronic devices, such as computer chips, solar cells and light-emitting diodes, all contain semiconductors. These are **elements** such as silicon, gallium and indium. To obtain the right electronic properties, these materials are 'doped' with small amounts of other elements, such as phosphorus and arsenic. Gallium arsenide or GaAs, is a very important semiconductor material. It is made by doping gallium with tiny amounts of very pure arsenic. Computer chips based on gallium arsenide are much quicker than those based on silicon and are used to make fast electronic devices like radar.

Doping semiconductors

Computer chips are made from semiconductors. These are electrical insulators when they are pure, but conduct electricity when tiny amounts of other elements are added to them. This process is called doping. Silicon doped with phosphorus or arsenic is called 'N-type silicon', while silicon doped with boron or gallium is called 'P-type silicon'. Both types are needed to make the millions of transistors in a silicon computer chip.

When light shines on gallium arsenide, some of its energy is converted into electricity. Solar cells containing gallium arsenide are used to power pocket calculators, satellites, road signs and public telephone kiosks. If electricity is passed through gallium arsenide, it gives off light. This makes it a useful material for making light-emitting diodes and semiconductor lasers. Light-emitting diodes (LEDs) are used in display screens for video recorders and other electrical equipment. They are more efficient than ordinary light bulbs and may eventually replace our traditional light fittings at home. CD and DVD players use semiconductor lasers containing gallium arsenide to read the digital information from disks.

◀ *This technician is holding a piece of gallium arsenide that will be used to make computer chips. Although they are faster than ordinary silicon chips, gallium arsenide chips are more expensive. Breathing apparatus and special clothing are needed during the manufacturing process to protect the technicians from poisonous arsenic fumes.*

Arsenic and old lumber

Small doses of arsenic **compounds** taken over time cause changes in skin colour, weakness and mental confusion. Single large doses cause vomiting, diarrhoea and death. There are relatively few modern uses of arsenic compounds and they are tightly controlled by law, so today we are unlikely to be poisoned by arsenic.

Arsenic the poisoner

Although arsenic is very poisonous – just a fifth of a gram can kill – arsenic compounds were widely used in the past. Fowler's solution, a popular tonic in Victorian times, contained potassium arsenite, KAs_2HO_4. It was prescribed for nearly every illness, although doctors needed to watch their patients carefully for signs of arsenic poisoning. 'Scheele's green' or copper arsenite, $CuAsHO_3$, was used in green inks for printing patterns on wallpaper and amazingly, as a green food colouring.

Politicians in ancient Rome were famous for using arsenic to remove people who stood between them and success. Arsenic has often been blamed for the suspicious deaths of rich and important people throughout history. Napoleon Bonaparte, exiled to a remote island called St Helena in 1815, eventually became ill with stomach cancer and died in 1821. It is possible that arsenic fumes from his wallpaper made his condition worse.

The Marsh test

An English chemist called James Marsh invented a sensitive test to detect arsenic poisoning in 1836. Sulphuric acid and zinc are added to the sample that is to be tested. Any arsenic present is converted into arsine gas, AsH_3. This breaks down into arsenic gas and hydrogen as it passes through a heated tube. The arsenic sublimes when it cools and forms shiny solid arsenic, which can be kept as evidence. Arsine is now used to dope silicon with arsenic to make N-type silicon for semiconductors.

Arsenic in the modern world

Leukaemia is a type of cancer in which the bone marrow makes too many white blood cells. Arsenic trioxide, As_2O_3, is sometimes used to treat leukaemia, especially if other medicines have been unsuccessful. It is also the most common arsenic compound used industrially and the major starting material for other arsenic compounds. Arsenic acid, H_3AsO_4, is used to sterilize soil before planting crops, while arsenic pentoxide, As_2O_5, and cacodylic acid, $C_2H_7AsO_2$, are weedkillers. The biggest single use for arsenic is in a wood preservative named chromated copper arsenate (CCA). CCA is a mixture of chromic acid, copper oxide and arsenic pentoxide. Timber is put into sealed containers and the CCA solution is forced into it under pressure. The pressure-treated wood resists attack by insects and fungi for many years.

This is Napoleon I of France (1769–1821), also called Napoleon Bonaparte. After his defeat at the Battle of Waterloo he was exiled by the British to St Helena, where he later died. The wallpaper in his room was dyed with Scheele's green, which produced poisonous arsenic fumes when damp and mouldy.

CHAPTER 6

Antimony

Antimony is a poisonous solid that exists in several forms. Metallic antimony is the most stable allotrope, consisting of shiny, blue-white crystals, but antimony also exists as yellow crystals and a black powder. Antimony only **reacts** with water or oxygen in the air when it is heated strongly, producing antimony oxide, Sb_2O_3, a white solid.

These are pieces of blue-white metallic antimony, which is the most stable form of the element. ▶

Burst pipes and antimony

Most substances contract or get smaller when they turn from a liquid into a solid, but some substances do the opposite. Water, for example, expands when it freezes. That is why water pipes can burst in winter if the water inside them freezes. Antimony is another substance that expands when it freezes. This property is useful when antimony is mixed with other metals. These antimony **alloys** expand to fill every nook and cranny when they solidify in moulds.

Ancient antimony

Antimony **compounds** have been used for thousands of years. Stibnite is antimony sulphide, Sb_2S_3, a black solid that easily leaves a mark when it is rubbed on another surface. It is the basis of a black eye-shadow called kohl, still used in some parts of the world. The chemical symbol for antimony, Sb, comes from *stibium*, the Latin word for antimony sulphide.

Not alone

Antimony is very rare in the Earth's crust and on average each tonne of rock contains only 5 g. It is thought that the name antimony may have come from the Greek words meaning 'not alone'. It is sometimes found on its own as a free **element**, but it is usually combined with sulphur to form stibnite, its most important **ore**. A bright red **mineral** called kermesite, Sb_2S_2O, is another important source of antimony. It is also recycled from car batteries. Over a hundred thousand tonnes of antimony is mined each year, nearly all of it in China.

Antimony and old iron

Antimony is easily obtained from its compounds. It is **extracted** from stibnite in two main stages. The stibnite is heated in air first, which converts it into antimony oxide, Sb_2O_3.

The word equation for converting stibnite into antimony oxide is:

$$\text{antimony sulphide} + \text{oxygen} \xrightarrow{\text{heat}} \text{antimony oxide} + \text{sulphur dioxide}$$

The oxygen is removed from the antimony oxide by heating it with scrap iron. The reaction forms molten antimony and molten iron sulphide. Antimony is denser than iron oxide, so it sinks to the bottom. It is piped away, cooled and solidified.

The word equation for producing antimony from antimony oxide:

$$\text{antimony oxide} + \text{iron} \xrightarrow{\text{heat}} \text{antimony} + \text{iron oxide}$$

◀ *A young Hindu girl (opposite) whose eyes have been decorated with black kohl eyeliner. Traditional kohl is made with antimony sulphide, lead sulphide or soot.*

Antimony is used to fuel starburst fireworks. When it burns, it produces white and gold glittery flames. It is often mixed with metals to produce **alloys** with useful properties, but most antimony is used as antimony oxide.

▲
Starburst fireworks like these usually contain antimony.

A type cast element

Lead is a soft metal, but becomes harder and stronger when alloyed with small amounts of antimony. Lead-antimony alloys are used in car batteries and bullets. Babbitt metals, named after their inventor Isaac Babbitt, are alloys used in car engines to reduce the friction between moving parts. Babbitt metals are typically 89 per cent tin, 4 per cent copper and 7 per cent antimony.

Type metal is an alloy that was widely used for printing books and newspapers. Its composition was about 50 per cent lead, 40 per cent tin and 10 per cent antimony. The tin made the lead hard and stopped it corroding. The antimony made it even harder and helped to give the letters a sharp outline by expanding into every part of the mould when the molten type metal solidified. Modern printing methods usually use other metals or plastics.

It makes you sick

Emetics are substances that make you vomit. Antimony potassium tartrate, also called 'tartar emetic', is a poisonous white powder that was used in the past as a medicine to treat people who had swallowed other poisons or sharp objects. Its own symptoms are similar to arsenic poisoning. Tartar emetic was effective in treating a tropical disease called schistosomiasis (pronounced 'shis-toe-so-my-a-siss'), caused by tiny worms that live in the veins around the liver and intestines. A modern medicine called praziquantel, which contains nitrogen, kills the worms without poisoning the patient. Antimony potassium tartrate is still used in the textile and leather industries as a mordant – a chemical that helps coloured dyes stick better.

◀ *This is a pair of Schistosoma worms (the female is the larger one and grows up to 2 cm long). They can infect people and attach themselves to the veins around the intestines, where they feed on blood. Antimony potassium tartrate was used in the past as a treatment to kill these worms.*

Antimony oxide

Antimony oxide is a white powder and the starting material for making the other antimony **compounds**. Glass often has a faint green tinge caused by impurities. Glass manufacturers may add small amounts of antimony oxide to their glass, which **reacts** with these impurities and removes tiny air bubbles. The biggest use of antimony oxide is in treating plastics and textiles to make them more fire resistant. It reacts with the fire retardant chemicals (usually chlorine or bromine compounds) to produce antimony chloride and antimony bromide, which help smother the flames. Many everyday objects are treated this way, including carpets, furniture and electrical appliances such as television sets.

Bismuth

Bismuth is a metal that consists of shiny crystals with a pink tinge. If it is heated strongly, it **reacts** with water and oxygen in the air to produce bismuth oxide, Bi_2O_3, a yellow solid. For a metal, bismuth is a poor conductor of heat and electricity. Copper is one of the best, conducting heat more than fifty times better than bismuth, and electricity more than sixty times. Metals such as iron are attracted to magnets, but others are actually repelled by them. Bismuth resists magnetic fields more than any other metal.

These are shiny crystals of bismuth metal.

Bismuth bergs

Bismuth, like antimony and water, expands when it freezes instead of contracting like most other substances. This property makes ice less **dense** than water and is why ice forms on the surface of puddles in winter. When molten bismuth cools down, bismuth crystals form on the surface of it, just like icebergs in the Arctic.

Discovery of bismuth

People have known about bismuth for over five hundred years, but thought it was just a variety of lead. It was used to harden the lead that made letter blocks for printing books. Claude Geoffroy, a French chemist, experimented with lead and bismuth in 1753 and demonstrated that they were really two different metals.

The white mass

The name bismuth comes to us in more than one step. It was first called 'weisse masse', which is German for white mass. This gradually changed to wismut, similar to bismut, its modern German name. The word was Latinized to 'bisemutum' to make it sound more learned and it later became bismuth.

Rare but we can get it

Bismuth is found as a free metal and in **minerals** such as bismite (bismuth oxide, Bi_2O_3) and bismuthinite (bismuth sulphide, Bi_2S_3). However, it is the rarest **group 5 element**, and on average there is only about one gram of bismuth in every forty tonnes of rock. Most deposits of bismuth minerals are too small to be mined at a profit, except in China, which produces half of the six thousand tonnes of bismuth mined each year. Elsewhere, bismuth is usually **extracted** as a by-product of lead **refining** and several complex steps are needed to separate bismuth from lead. Bismuth is also found in the waste material left behind when copper is refined.

Uses of bismuth

Shotgun pellets are made from lead because it is very **dense**. However it is also poisonous and can badly affect animals that swallow any pellets left behind. Bismuth is almost as dense as lead (it is next to lead in the **periodic table**) but it is not poisonous. This means that bismuth is an 'environmentally-friendly' replacement for lead in shotgun pellets. They are, however, three times more expensive than steel pellets, which are also used instead of lead.

A hunter, calling for ducks with his yellow Labrador retriever dog. Bismuth is used as an 'environmentally-friendly' replacement for lead in shotgun pellets.

Mouldy metals

Metal parts are often made by a process called casting. Molten metal is poured into a mould. It cools and solidifies, producing a metal copy. However, molten metals usually shrink as they solidify, so they eventually pull away from the inside of the mould and the fine detail is not reproduced.

In contrast, bismuth expands by 3.3 per cent when it solidifies. When metals are mixed with bismuth to produce **alloys**, they expand very slightly as they solidify and push into all the small holes and corners in a mould, producing a very good-quality cast. This is particularly useful when a factory needs to make exact metal copies of pottery, plastic or metal objects for making new moulds.

Machining metals

Cast steel and aluminium are machined into shape using tools. If the metals contain small amounts of bismuth, they become easier to machine, which saves money. The cutting and shaping tools last longer and the machining itself takes less time. The metal parts may also be held in place by bismuth alloys with low melting points while they are being machined.

Fuses and fires

Bismuth alloys have low melting points, so they are used in electrical fuses. These are electrical components needed in the circuit, usually in the plug and main fuse box, to protect us if electrical devices are defective. When drills, hairdryers and other electrical devices become faulty, they may draw too much current. If the current becomes too high, the metal in the fuse heats up and melts, which breaks the circuit and stops the electricity flowing. Bismuth alloys are also used in the automatic valves for sprinkler systems that are installed in the ceilings of shopping centres and other public buildings. If a fire breaks out, the heat melts the bismuth alloy plug in the valve. This lets water flow through the valve, forming a fine mist that helps put out the fire.

How low can you go?

Melting points of bismuth alloys may be lower than the melting points of the individual metals. Bismuth melts at 272 °C and tin melts at 232 °C, but a mixture of 58 per cent bismuth and 42 per cent tin melts at just 138 °C. Alloys of bismuth, tin, indium, cadmium and lead may melt at less than 60 °C.

Most bismuth is used in **alloys**, but just over a third of it is used in bismuth **compounds**. Bismuth oxychloride, BiOCl, for instance, is a white solid used in 'metallic' car paints. It forms small, flat crystals that scatter light in all directions, giving the paint a shiny finish. Fish scales are sometimes added to lipstick, eye-shadow and nail varnish to give them a glowing 'pearlescent' appearance. Thankfully, bismuth oxychloride crystals achieve the same effect in cosmetics without the fish!

◀ *Bismuth oxychloride is added to cosmetics to give them a smooth and attractive appearance.*

Going hot and cold with bismuth

You probably use a thermometer to measure temperature. However, temperature can be measured using a thermocouple. This is formed from a pair of wires, each made of a different metal, welded together at one end. When the thermocouple is warmed up, a small electrical voltage is produced. The hotter the wires get, the bigger the voltage. Bismuth makes an especially good negative wire in thermocouples and is often used with antimony, another **group** 5 **element**.

In 1834, French physicist Jean Peltier discovered that thermocouples could work in reverse. If electricity is passed through two different metals joined together, one end gets hot while the other end gets cold. This is called the Peltier effect and is used to make refrigerators with no moving parts. Modern devices use bismuth selenide and bismuth telluride. They are expensive and inefficient, but small and quiet, which makes them ideal for wine coolers, hotel minibars and cool boxes for cars.

Tummy trouble

While our food is being digested, extra water is added to it from the stomach and small intestine. This water is normally absorbed back into our bodies in the large intestine. Sometimes bacteria and spicy food can interfere with the normal working of the large intestine. This stops the water being absorbed, so we get runny faeces or diarrhoea as a result. Bismuth salicylate (pronounced sa-lissy-late) is a medicine that is used to treat diarrhoea and reduces the symptoms of an upset stomach.

Bismuth catalysts

Bismuth phosphomolybdate (pronounced 'fos-fo mo-lib-date') is a **catalyst** used in the manufacture of acrylonitrile. This is an important chemical needed to make plastics such as artificial rubber and acrylonitrile-butadiene-styrene (ABS). ABS is a tough plastic used to make helmets, suitcases and car parts. Acrylonitrile is also an ingredient in the manufacture of nylon and acrylic fibres for carpets and clothing.

◀ The safety helmets these men are wearing are made from a tough plastic called acrylonitrile-butadiene-styrene (ABS). To make acrylonitrile, which is a chemical used to manufacture ABS, a catalyst called bismuth phosphomolybdate is needed.

Poisonous acrylonitrile

*Acrylonitrile, C_3H_3N, contains another group 5 element, nitrogen. It is made by **reacting** propene (a substance made from crude oil), ammonia and oxygen together at 450 °C. Acrylonitrile is sometimes used to kill insect pests in tobacco crops, but many countries have banned this practice because it may cause cancer.*

Find out more about the group 5 elements

The table below contains some information about the
properties of the **group 5 elements**.

Element	Symbol	Atomic number	Melting point (°C)	Boiling point (°C)	State at 25 °C	Density at 25 °C (g/cm³)
nitrogen	N	7	−210	−196	gas	0.00115
phosphorus	P	15	44	280	solid	1.82
arsenic	As	33	817*	616*	solid	5.78
antimony	Sb	51	631	1635	solid	6.70
bismuth	Bi	83	272	1560	solid	9.75

*If you look carefully, it seems that arsenic's melting point is
higher than its boiling point. It only looks like this because
they are measured at different pressures. At ordinary pressure,
arsenic sublimes (turns directly from a solid to a gas) at
616 °C. To get liquid arsenic, we have to heat it to 817 °C
at twenty-eight times the normal pressure.

Compounds
These tables show you the chemical formulae of most of the
compounds mentioned in this book. For example, ammonia has
the formula NH_3. This means it is made from one nitrogen **atom**
and three hydrogen atoms, joined together by chemical **bonds**.

Bismuth compounds

Bismuth compounds	formula
bismuth oxide	Bi_2O_3
bismuth oxychloride	$BiOCl$
bismuth phosphomolybdate	$Bi_9PMo_{12}O_{52}$
bismuth salicylate	$BiC_7H_5O_4$
bismuth selenide	Bi_2Se_3
bismuth sulphide	Bi_2S_3
bismuth telluride	Bi_2Te_3

Nitrogen compounds	formula
acrylonitrile	C_3H_3N
ammonia	NH_3
ammonium carbonate	$(NH_4)2CO_3$
ammonium hydroxide	NH_4OH
ammonium nitrate	NH_4NO_3
ammonium phosphate	$(NH_4)3PO_4$
ammonium sulphate	$(NH_4)2SO_4$
amyl nitrate	$C_5H_{11}NO_3$
butyl nitrate	$C_4H_9NO_3$
dinitrotoluene	$CH_3C_6H_3(NO_2)_2$
nitric acid	HNO_3
nitrogen dioxide	NO_2
nitrogen monoxide	NO
nitroglycerine	$C_3H_5(ONO_2)_3$
nitrous acid	HNO_2
potassium nitrate	KNO_3
praziquantel	$C_{19}H_{24}N_2O_2$
sodium nitrate	$NaNO_3$
trinitrotoluene	$CH_3C_6H_2(NO_2)_3$

Arsenic compounds	formula
arsenic acid	H_3AsO_4
arsenic pentoxide	As_2O_5
arsenic sulphide	As_2S_3
arsenic trioxide	As_2O_3
arsine	AsH_3
cacodylic acid	$C_2H_7AsO_2$
copper arsenite	$CuAsHO_3$
iron arsenic sulphide	$FeAsS$
potassium arsenite	KAs_2HO_4

Find out more continued

Phosphorus compounds

Phosphorous compounds	formula
calcium phosphate	$Ca_3(PO_4)_2$
iron phosphate	$FePO_4$
phosphoric acid	H_3PO_4
phosphorus pentoxide	P_2O_5
phosphorus sulphide	P_4S_3
sodium tripolyphosphate	$Na_5P_3O_{10}$

Antimony compounds

Antimony compounds	formula
antimony bromide	$SbBr_3$
antimony chloride	$SbCl_3$
antimony oxide	Sb_2O_3
antimony sulphide (stibnite)	Sb_2S_3
kermesite	Sb_2S_2O
potassium antimony tartrate	$KSbC_4H_4O_7$

Other compounds

Other compounds	formula
butane	C_4H_{10}
calcium silicate	$CaSiO_3$
calcium sulphate	$CaSO_4$
carbon dioxide	CO_2
carbon monoxide	CO
copper oxide	CuO
glycerol	$C_3H_5(OH)_3$
iron oxide	Fe_2O_3
iron sulphide	FeS
natural gas (methane)	CH_4
potassium chlorate	$KClO_3$
propane	C_3H_8
propene	C_3H_6
sand (silica)	SiO_2
sulphur dioxide	SO_2
water	H_2O

Acids	formula
arsenic acid	H_3AsO_4
cacodylic acid	$C_2H_7AsO_2$
chromic acid	H_2CrO_4
hydrochloric acid	HCl
hydrobromic acid	HBr
nitric acid	HNO_3
nitrous acid	HNO_2
phosphoric acid	H_3PO_4
sulphuric acid	H_2SO_4

Glossary

alloy mixture of two or more metals or mixture of a metal and a non-metal. Alloys are often more useful than one pure metal on its own.

atom smallest particle of an element that has the properties of that element. Atoms contain smaller particles called subatomic particles.

atomic number number of protons in the nucleus of an atom. It is also called the proton number. No two elements have the same atomic number.

bond force that joins atoms together

catalyst substance that speeds up reactions without getting used up

compound substance made from the atoms of two or more elements, joined together by chemical bonds. Compounds can be broken down into simpler substances and have different properties from the elements in them. For example, water is a liquid at room temperature, but it is made from two gases, hydrogen and oxygen.

density mass of a substance compared to its volume. To work out the density of a substance, you divide its mass by its volume. Substances with a high density feel very heavy for their size.

detonator device needed to set off an explosive

distillation method used to separate a liquid or gas from a mixture. It works because the liquid or gas has a lower boiling point than the rest of the mixture.

DNA (deoxyribonucleic acid) long, complex chemical that carries the genetic information and is the substance of inheritance for almost all living things

electron subatomic particle with a negative electric charge. Electrons are found around the nucleus of an atom.

element substance made from one type of atom. Elements cannot be broken down into simpler substances. All substances are made from one or more elements.

extract remove a chemical from a mixture of chemicals

fertilizer chemical that gives plants the elements required for healthy growth

fractional distillation method of separating mixtures of two or more liquids. It works because liquids have different boiling points.

group vertical column of elements in the periodic table. Elements in a group have similar properties.

liquefy turn a gas into a liquid by cooling or pressurizing it

mineral substance that is found naturally, but does not come from animals or plants. Metal ores and limestone are examples of minerals.

molecule smallest particle of an element or compound that exists by itself. A molecule is usually made from two or more atoms joined together by chemical bonds.

neutralize when an acid and an alkali or a base react together. The solution made is neutral, which means it is not acidic or alkaline.

neutron subatomic particle with no electric charge. Neutrons are found in the nucleus of an atom.

nuclear reaction reaction involving the nucleus of an atom. Radiation is produced in nuclear reactions.

nucleus part of an atom made from protons and neutrons. It has a positive electric charge and is found at the centre of the atom.

ore substance that contains minerals from which metals or other elements can be taken out and purified

oxidizing agent chemical that can add oxygen to an element or compound in a chemical reaction. Oxidizing agents are also called oxidants.

period horizontal row of elements in the periodic table

periodic table table in which all the known elements are arranged into groups and periods

product substance made in a chemical reaction

propellant gas that forces the contents out of an aerosol can

proton subatomic particle with a positive electric charge. Protons are found in the nucleus of an atom.

reaction chemical change that produces new substances

refining removing impurities from a substance to make it pure. It can also mean separating the different substances in a mixture, for example, in oil refining.

subatomic particle particle smaller than an atom, such as a proton, a neutron or an electron

vacuum empty space containing very little air or none at all

Timeline

arsenic discovered	1250	Albertus Magnus
phosphorus discovered	1669	Hennig Brand
antimony discovered	1707	Nicolas Lémery
bismuth discovered	1753	Claude Geoffroy
nitrogen discovered	1772	Daniel Rutherford
nitroglycerine discovered	1846	Ascanio Sobrero
dynamite invented	1867	Alfred Nobel
Ostwald process for making nitric acid patented	1902	William Ostwald
Haber process for making ammonia developed	1909	Fritz Haber

Further reading and useful websites

Books

Knapp, Brian, *The Elements* series, particularly, *Nitrogen and Phosphorus* (Atlantic Europe Publishing Co., 1996)

Oxlade, Chris, *Chemicals in Action* series, particularly, *Acids and Bases* (Heinemann Library, 2002)

Oxlade, Chris, *Chemicals in Action* series, particularly, *Elements and Compounds* (Heinemann Library, 2002)

Websites

WebElements™
http://www.webelements.com
An interactive periodic table crammed with information and photographs.

Proton Don
http://www.funbrain.com/periodic
The fun periodic table quiz!

Mineralogy Database
http://www.webmineral.com
Useful information about minerals, including colour photographs and information about their chemistry.

DiscoverySchool
http://school.discovery.com/clipart
Help for science projects homework and free science clip art.

BBC Science
http://www.bbc.co.uk/science
Quizzes, news, information and games about all areas of science.

Creative Chemistry
http://www.creative-chemistry.org.uk
An interactive chemistry site with fun practical activities, quizzes, puzzles and more.

Index

Titles in the *Periodic Table* series include:

Hardback   0 431 16995 0

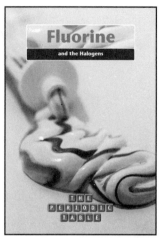

Hardback   0 431 16997 7

Hardback   0 431 16998 5

Hardback   0 431 16996 9

Hardback   0 431 16994 2

Hardback   0 431 16999 3

Find out about the other titles in this series on our website www.heinemann.co.uk/library